A GARDEN *of* ANCHORS

A GARDEN *of* ANCHORS
SELECTED POEMS

JOY KOGAWA

mosaic press

National Library of Canada Cataloguing in Publication Data

A Garden of anchors : selected poems / by Joy Kogawa

ISBN 0-88962-808-4

1. Title

PS8521.O44G37 2003   C811'.54   C2003-901053-8
PR9199.3.K63G37 2003

Published by Mosaic Press, offices and warehouse at 1252 Speers Road, Units 1 and 2, Oakville, Ontario, L6L 5N9, Canada and Mosaic Press, PMB 145, 4500 Witmer Industrial Estates, Niagara Falls, NY, 14305-1386, U.S.A.

Mosaic Press acknowledges the assistance of the Canada Council and the Department of Canadian Heritage, Government of Canada for their support of our publishing programme.

Mosaic Press in Canada:
1252 Speers Road, Units 1 & 2,
Oakville, Ontario
L6L 5N9
Phone/Fax: 905-825-2130
mosaicpress@on.aibn.com

Mosaic Press in U.S.A.:
4500 Witmer Industrial Estates
PMB 145, Niagara Falls, NY
14305-1386
Phone/Fax: 1-800-387-8992
mosaicpress@on.aibn.com

Le Conseil des Arts   The Canada Council
du Canada   for the Arts

www.mosaic-press.com

to the one i don't know
exactly anymore
but a little better
than i did before

Joy

Other Books by Joy Kogawa

The Splintered Moon, 1967
A Choice of Dreams, 1974
Jericho Road, 1977,
Obasan, 1981
Woman in the Woods, 1985
Naomi's Road, 1986
Itsuka, 1992
The Rain Ascends, 1995, revised 2003
A Song of Lilith, 2000

Acknowledgements

Thanks to Patrick Woodcock for his editorial assistance; Chris Kurata and Ian Sowton for their help in selecting the poems; Robert Burns for his excellent design assistance; Natasha Hunt for her care in designing the text.

A special thanks to Aiko Suzuki for her mixed media cover image,"Homage to a Nisei," honouring her nisei father, Carr Suzuki. The work features bamboo, a gift from her father's garden.

These poems, written mostly in the 60's and 70's owe their new lease on life to Howard Aster and the people of Mosaic Press.

Table of Contents

Cedar Incense

Forest Creatures

Water Garden

Cedar Incense

Ancestors' Graves in Kurakawa

down down across the open sea to shikoku
to story book island of mist and mystery
by train and bus through remote mountain villages
following my father's boyhood backwards
retracing the mountain path he crossed on rice husk slippers
his dreams still intact, his flight perpetual
back down the steep red mountain path
to the high hillside grave of my ancestors
grey and green ferns hang down
edging my faint beginnings with shades
maintaining muteness in a wordless flickering
the hiddenness stretches beyond my reach
strange dew drops through cedar incense
and i greet the dead who smile through trees
accepting the pebbles that melt through my eyes.

from *A Choice of Dreams*

Descent into Smog

bumpy chowder clouds our descent
into forecast of smoke haze
sun angles away to airport scene
the tokyo trot
much bowing, many bow legs
grey kimono emerges, tightness, anxiety –
my aunt has helmetitis, or is it
just a temporary helmet she puts on
when something has to be done –
like standing in hard hat areas
meeting north american strangers –
nervous hands ask
what's your name, child?
curiosa? cursiosa?
schedule, purpose,
what's the game?
home is where the heart is, i feel
which is an open question
these wounding days
she escorts me through black exhaust
hurtling smog, open toilet smells
jerky conversation, i cut the automatic
and turn to manual breathing, watch the
red alert in my temple and
try to adjust

from *A Choice of Dreams*

Zen Graveyard

thick night mist
mountainside, stone ghosts
graves rising in steps into trees
strange familiarity
small girl once upon a time
red and white kimono, short hair
not here perhaps but somewhere
a wild boar perhaps, perhaps not
waterfall, a sound not unlike a violin
bell tone of insect, praying mantis nearby
curled coloured snails on mossy trees –
to have to stand alone here
in this almost place when
once upon a time, perhaps –

from *A Choice of Dreams*

On Hearing Japanese Haiku

throat blossoms to sounds
sama zama no mono
stirrings in the sandy fibres of my flesh
and these ancient fingers
gardening

from *A Choice of Dreams*

A Tempo

lost in a maze of corridors
with a useless map
streets the width of hallways
and basin size backyard gardens
bow legged women churn the
everywhere falling dust
brown air brown arms brown earth
a boy plays a bach fugue
with the piano
almost on the sidewalk
a patchy rooster
squats in a cramped cage

from *A Choice of Dreams*

Glances

at first glance
the tea ceremony
seems a tedious discipline

on second glance i see
tiny pock mark scars
on the back of a hand

healing moxibustion?
punishment by burning?
(i remember the child
in slocan, weeping...)

we lift ancient tea bowls
taste the frothy green tea
empty our minds

from *A Choice of Dreams*

This Is a Clearing

this is a clearing
there is the forest
this is the forest
there is the clearing –
my gentle relatives are standing in dark sunlight
whispered about with monumental propriety
gathering on the occasion of a wedding
to impale and dismember a missing relative
chanting a creed "we belong we belong"
i stand on the edge
if i enter the forest i am lost
if i enter the clearing i am still lost
i move in a direction
chanting a creed "we belong we belong"
a large tree cracks

from *A Choice of Dreams*

On Meeting the Clergy of the Holy Catholic Church in Osaka

heralded into a belly-swelling bladder-bloating banquet
where the excessive propriety is hard on the digestion
elegant ladies in kimonos and holy men with holier manners
bow and re-bow in strict pecking order
munch the meal and mouth polite belching and
rush at flood tide to the integrated toilet
where men still proper and black suited in a row
stand toes out and eyes down in syncopated gush
while ladies in kimonos mince by without blush or bellow
and i follow snuffling to hide a guffaw though
why i should laugh – which reminds me
at the osaka zoo my friend kept pointing out
the peeing fox and the baboon's purple bum and such
asking how to say these things in english
and i tried to explain about the odd canadians
who have no bread and butter words
to describe these ordinary things

from *A Choice of Dreams*

For the Annual Service of Thanks that Kyoto Was Spared the Bomb

for the fact that this temple was not bombed
and these dragons still stand guard –
for this network of lanes on the city's edges
shaded by ancient trees
for this pre-meiji pond and its family of rocks
this still living and aging thatch roofed house
for kinkakuji and ginkakuji and countless wooden buildings
for these and other treasures still preserved
we give thanks oh military strategists
and wish a happy unbirthday to you kyoto
pollyanna city of grace and gratitude –
a few miles away in hiroshima
the wide boulevard in front of peace park
is jammed on international peace day
with a new generation of students
who feel they know what to say

from *A Choice of Dreams*

The Chicken Killing

down the dusty country lane
along drying rice propped in lines like soldiers on parade
and blue pantalooned people in the distance pantomiming –
two men standing, three crouched in ritual stance
sweat cloths around foreheads, open undershirts, black cloth boots
one with knife, one grinning toothless –
plump white fluttering held feet first
conveniently drains its veins as it struggles
then flung aside, leaps through the air –
i walk past down the trembling road
tasting the sound of dusty feet and
feeling on my neck the slight saltiness of a question –
i am dangling feet first from the sky
– perhaps if i do not struggle –

from *A Choice of Dreams*

Public Bath

daily to the ofuro
with basin, soap, towel and thirty-five yen
with neighbours strangers and friends
to boil away altogether
all together in the bath
and with wash cloth rolled tight
as hard ball pumice stone
scrape and scrub each other's backs
already lobster red from steam
squat and flob flob with soap
and splash and soak again
till steam and dumpling soft
we merge as one warm vat
of boiled jelly fish
all our offensive scabs and irritations
rolled off in communal banter –
would that this could be exported home
and politicians and business men and sons
could meet together in the public bath
to batter and scrub each other raw
and dissolve the ills of the day
and my frozen neighbours in suburbia
grannies and babies and mothers
and children all wrapped in skin
could melt at the end of their day

from *A Choice of Dreams*

Saturday Night in Osaka

strolling along the stretching saturday night streets of osaka
between osaka station and the dark corners of the ywca
jostled by mini car and multi-legged man
in narrow lane of lantern light and noise
screeching brakes of unoiled bicycles
pachinko parlors, glowing purple escalators
with my japanese face in my dragon lady disguise
english like a dagger in my teeth
flashing out against lonely challenging men
"be my friend, miss? have some tea?"
shrug (i don't speak japanese anyway, kid)
i saunter back to the safety of the y
and glumly brush my fangs with toothpaste
like a million other antiseptic inhibited biddies
who fear to look ridiculous or worse
and for the rest of the evening
thumb through a japanese-english dictionary
and listen to the man in the next alley
as he directs the traffic of a swaggering saturday night
shouting "orai orai orai" (all right all right)
among the centipedes and dragonflies and exploding neon lights

from *A Choice of Dreams*

Day of the Bride

the day of the bride dawns
through layers of white plaster skin
and multi-sashed kimono
head made huge by lacquered hair –
she is swept ashore in her glass bottle
white and tight as a folded paper message
eyes hidden in a swirl of green boughs
she moves like a mannequin
maneuvered by centuries of ceremony
under the weight of speech and incantation
a wail of priests and watching families
beside rows of low tables
with small triangles of paper
congratulatory slits of squid and curls of seaweed
then kneeling at the bend of a fresh memory
she is discarded by her heavy day
and is plunged into a twentieth century
tiny apartment daily stream
as a barely visible folded paper speck

from *A Choice of Dreams*

Rush Hour Tokyo

pelted shapeless in rush hour crush
bicycle pedestrian car cart jostling
hip to bumper, wheel to toe
police whistle siren scream
political speech neon
flashing particle people blur
past ticket takers the world's
most accurate mechanical men
pummel down subway stairs
and shove heave oh canada my
home and native land give
me land lots of land

from *A Choice of Dreams*

Policeman at Yokozuka

raining and as usual
lost and sleepy and not
knowing where to go find
a police station
ask to rest and sleep
and when i wake i'm
covered by a blanket --
rice balls beside me
and a policeman with a
constant smile watches as i
wake and wipe the dry
spit off my cheek -- we
talk and all the while
the sun steams the rain
to mist and all the
policemen in all the world
are as warm as the
green tea he pours for us
and finally when he asks
to see my passport i
know it is not to
mutilate

Night in a Boat between Beppu and Kobe

at least three hundred men and five women
in the lower section of this rocking boat
squeezed body to body on the thrumming floor
some men fully dressed in underwear
drinking sake, playing cards and singing
some already snoring open mouthed
stiff on their backs beside each other
i squinch into my corner and lie down
too curious to sleep too proper to be comfortable
the question of the unalert moment
propping open my east-west eyes
a man's foot is on my buttock help
but he seems to be asleep
and i am watchtower
witnessing on a busy corner
with a pamphlet in my hand
that says, awake, lick the crust from your eyelids
watch and wait (it's a sightseeing trip)
i begin the taking off and putting on of masks
smiling carefully at the man on my other side
and frowning at the demons dancing
gleeing to my bright dark imaginings
by morning i am in a stupor
having dramatized my corner all night
but can only report that there is no action
in having a strange man's foot on one's buttock
in a crowded overnight boat in japan –
on the deck and in the first class cabins
other passengers have been viewing
what some say is the world's
most scenic inland sea

from *A Choice of Dreams*

Newspaper Item: Student Suicide

in soot silence bamboo grows
tree surgeons discuss the cause of wood rot
pines point crooked arms to the sky

rain drops the sky down in grey pieces and
darkness moves with the urgency of flight
from a bad dream

everyday
the newspaper reports
a bad dream

tomorrows were mountaintops
sculptured pines
and wind-pruned asymmetry

a student went chestnut picking
and heard the "mim mim"
of an autumn cicada

from *A Choice of Dreams*

Dwarf Trees

out of the many small embarrassments of the day
grew a miniature personality
leafing itself gingerly in whatever genuine smile
it recognized in the thick undergrowth
dwarf trees planted in a fertile gentleness
beside lush vegetation and sheltering green fans
grew angular and stunted in a constant adjustment to cutting
horns of new growths sprouted
to bleed into warts and tiny anxieties
glances of disapproval felt as sharply
as salivating fangs tore at limbs
men developed into twisted sculptures of endurance
bowing and smiling in civilized anger
and old women pruned daily into careful beauty
glanced away in a cultivated shyness
hiding smiles with humpbacked hands
symbolizing by small gestures
tiny treasures from a hidden childhood

from *A Choice of Dreams*

Lost Man at the Tourist Information Centre

wide eyed and childlike the lost one comes
bulbous nosed australian, outstandingly fat
flailing his stubby wings at all the strange
bobbing creatures in his way
booms at prim hostess
"i've been in japan a fortnight
and haven't eaten a good australian meal
i'm almost starving to death"
japanese blinks at the bulk in front
no mirth
clucking efficiency she flutters
on her perch at the lost and found booth
roots through directories for the choicest grub
bobs and bows the waddler on his way
into the mad taxi traffic
of the ginza barnyard
where he bellows like a baby ox
among intensely polite
and earnest jack-in-a-boxes

from *A Choice of Dreams*

School in the Woods

north korean school in kyoto woods, sports day
blue white uniformed young people,
military music, red star in white circle
a poster of a soldier wielding a long gun
another of a toothy u.s. devil
bayoneting an oriental man

a small boy in front of me eats a rice ball
and watches me with a careful stare
it is an autumn day in kyoto
full of tiny coloured maple leaves

back home some mother glimpses
bayonets in the air, turns off the tv
tucks her child into bed

from *A Choice of Dreams*

Moon over Uchiko

9:00 p.m. evening lullaby and gong
half hymn, half child's play song
over this mountain village
cicadas and crickets chirp whirr
acorns drop down with soft thuds –
i slip through softly sliding doorways
of matchstick wood and paper
to where my aunt in grey kimono
sits in a rock garden by a pond
beneath a white moon without hint of footprint –
shuffling pigeon toed my aunt of much bowing
descends upon my feet with great graciousness
clutches my arms and clings
suspended in the ether of my deciding
"stay longer stay longer stay stay"
she opens for me her collection of memories
– my father as a child gathering cow dung for the garden
– my grandmother accused of farting in school
and weeping in a tub for a day –
she tugs me towards her dry hollows
and i am deformed with etiquette
as my plastic arms encircle her
and melt in the heat of her tears –
the steel beam in my back cracks
as she leans heavily crying and sighing –
i begin the countdown – words to prop her
a cane for her to clutch "dear aunt
i am beginning to learn how better to lie"
she bends double as i depart in a gust of metal
rocketing the willowy trees bare in her october garden

from *A Choice of Dreams*

At Jindaiji Temple Fishing Pond

rooting for the smooth grey fish
being hooked and snared by laughing child
and powerless in the cool grey weather
to leap out of one element into another
wishing only to avoid the death
of being hooked on my gills by some cosmic child
and gleefully serenaded into a pebbly blackness
of some gourmet's solar intestines –
saying with vehemence i am a fish
and will die the death of a cold grey fish
near my familiar mountain waterfall
but even here fishermen dangle
worms on hooks into the stream of my peace
to pull me up into the rare deadly air –
above the surface of my sky
pure white seagulls circle
and i know that if i bite
it is for a devouring and an end
to the swift flash of my dark
sporting body beneath the bumpy waves
but what does it matter to rot here or there
if i cannot will away this child
and the expansive smiling of his father

from *A Choice of Dreams*

Insomnia in a Ryokan

what? no sound down the corridor?
no foot falls, flap flap slippered slap
or patter thud of plastic sole?
only this smooth wooden floor
only this faint echo of radio, tv, faraway drama
flamenco dancers in dreams
hints of snoring through hotel walls
what more can one ask?
a leap to a naked drum beat?
a primitive frenzy of touch?
one can insist on footsteps
one can insist on dancing
look, the midnight can take shape
slender fingerlings of dancing
can cavort down corridors
hah!
i'll leap into your snoring
shout out my english subtitles
"let me in!"
if you could understand my fairy tales

from *A Choice of Dreams*

Flower Arranger

among the weedy steel structures
and frenetic blossoming of factories
i found a blind flower arranger
in a sketch of a room
dipping a drop of water
onto an opening petal
of a tiny not quite flowering bud –
with his fingertips
he placed gentleness in the air
and everywhere among the blowing weeds
he moved with his outstretched hands
touching the air
with his transient dew

from *A Choice of Dreams*

Black Skirt of Mount Fuji in Rain

almost late for the tomei bus to nagoya
spot the one empty seat and sit down
by the bleary eyed man the others had shunned
he takes out his suntory whisky, peels off
the plastic top, nudges me tentatively –
we travel on through several stages of misunderstanding
me, anxious to see the countryside
and listening to the recorded announcements –
"mount fuji to the left" the voice says
i peer out the window – pouring rain –
the mountain exists in my imagination
the next announcement "i'm sorry
when you are in such a hurry
to have to stop for refueling"
a lunchgirl arrives calling
"bother is being done, is lunch desired?"
politeness all over this apologetic country
and i had to get old suntory
i decide to do a mount fuji
and obliterate myself in mist
"yes" i say in english to the nudger
"what would you like?"

from *A Choice of Dreams*

Goddess of Mercy

autumn and not one leaf
on grey white sand constant ripple
of pebbly sea rock garden –
the goddess of mercy rests her bronze ankle
on her knee, unmoving and perfect –
i slash the air like a medieval executioner
at a mosquito swooping past my face
and across the sand sea of eternity
into the safety of the thick moss
my black blood in its belly –
across the smoggy sky, two jets crisscross
from the highway a whine of traffic
swells and fades

from *A Choice Of Dreams*

Girls in the Ginza

bleach me brown or bleach me blonde
the japanese girl demands
surrounded by caucasian mannequins –
she begs the plastic surgeon man
to snip the muscles of her slitty eyes
lift her nose, plump her breasts –
false eyelashes and latest fashions on
she walks around the ginza
not quite who she wants to be
her thick black hair rusting
under the peroxide rain

from *A Choice of Dreams*

Gift Giving and Obligation

note from the lonely spaces –
beware the kindness, the smothering places
of gifts piled on gifts –
"this is nothing – just a token"

as eyes murmur pleasure at your refusal –
refuse yet more profusely
till finally, humbly bowing
acknowledge obligation

or leave abruptly
in your barbaric western way
to the sound of the chanting
"weight, weight, we love you"

from *A Choice of Dreams*

Child Eichmann

the orders were to kill the kittens
and obedience was the first commandment
he took the first, still sac enclosed
a slippery blackness in his kitten size palm
and drowned it in a pail of water
felt its pawing with needle thin scratchings
watched it swimming, mewing, gaping –
life comes, goes, mouths open, close
the small sounds are buried in the night's
darkness and wild dreaming – "okaasan!"
she blames the persimmons and squats him
over the open toilet which has not yet
been cleaned by the monthly manure collector
the smell from his bowels fills the house

from *A Choice of Dreams*

Bamboo Broom

at the shinto shrine
grey green stone lanterns
scowling chinese lion dogs
protecting against irreverence and intrusion
triangular tiny white porcelain foxes
grains of rice placed at the feet
of the rice god, oinari-san
a record playing "dinah won't you blow – "
a woman tossing a ten yen piece
into a wooden box, bowing her head
clapping her hands twice
moss, water, tiny plum trees
PEACE cigarettes on the path
another brand called HOPE
(is there one called GOODWILL?)
a woman with a bamboo broom
sweeping the ground
a tour of school children
in navy blue english uniforms
crowding in past the lion dogs
(swish swish swish)

from *A Choice of Dreams*

At Maruyama Park, Kyoto

up stone steps to dark temple at night
a wail of flickering lights around stone statues
centuries of looking down
water drips, moss clings
a tiny brown frog leaps
splash
into a pool

from *A Choice of Dreams*

At Shinjuku Park, November 19

through the park
in autumn, warm leaf time
with transient foot
it being time to go home
time, swear, to go home
and some loudspeaker plays
auld lang syne
yanking a raindrop out of nowhere
we trudge through the song
carrying the ocean with us
above us, seagulls cross
on a path of splashing waves
brushing aside whatever spray
clings to their wings –
little point in delaying departure
now the time to go has come
in the middle of this dance
in this autumn morning
i cling to my flight

from *A Choice of Dreams*

Early Morning Stage

a messy city
early morning and traffic whine mosquito whine
toilet smell, cricket and dog sounds
corrugated cardboard sheets
oddly, a cow mooing? a rooster crowing?
the mosquito jabs my arm
i pull myself out of heavy futon
step over tatami to hallway
slip on slip off slippers
cloth slippers for hall
plastic slippers for toilet
squat foetal fashion over the flushless hole –
through the floor level window vent
the sounds of feet pass
outside in the pre-dawn grey and constant smog
early morning scuttlers disappear
pigeons flutter with the debris
a man with a fist full of red flowers
urinates against a bush
a girl with an easel paints a school building
a loudspeaker above the school door plays
the "what a friend we have in jesus" march
bicycles with primitive brakes screech
ladies hang futon over railings
a roast potato man
pulls his wooden cart and calls
"yaki imo" through his scratchy loudspeaker –
i remember that corner of tokyo
but now i open my eyes
to a suburban white walled house in ottawa
early morning and a long silence
as if the curtain has just gone up
or down and something electrifying has just happened
or is about to happen and the day has begun

or ended – it is up to me to decide
i am director producer playwright or
actress on stage needing
laughing lessons and i'm thinking
of firing her – the audience has disappeared
and the walls intrude –
the mail truck crunches by

from *A Choice of Dreams*

Trunk in the Attic

rummaging through the old metal trunk in
the attic above the church hall in coaldale, alberta –
the trunk which traveled with us
through the world war 2 evacuation of japanese
from the west coast – filled then with dishes
dresses and assorted treasures
and now only half full of baby dresses
an old tablecloth, invitation to dinner xmas 1915 –
my white haired mother hands me
a deep purple kimono bought
in some vaguely remembered girlhood
of apple shaped pears and sweet chestnuts
and utterly unabandoned babies
asleep on their mothers' backs –
i take the memories from her tapered fingers
fold her hands which no longer cling
close the lid of the trunk –
the sharp whiff of mothballs fades from the room
and she turns to climb down the stairs
one step at a time
rubbing the mucus steadily
from her cataract covered eyes

from *A Choice of Dreams*

Forest Creatures

Bird Song

flung from nests
in late spring
and ordered to fly
or die we are
weaned to the air

in this our flight
lord in this long
fall the call
is clear

to rise to sunlight
through springtime
storms and wars with
wings grown strong

but here these wind-trimmed
unformed bones
and tiny beaks

that sing
inaudible songs

from *Woman in the Woods*

Poem for My Enemies

the will to love you lurks
like the ghost of christmas-to-come
with its armful of funerals

the wind stretches fingers
seeking edges in the
silent watching night

it is here in the waiting
that angels come rushing
in like fools

from *Jericho Road*

Where There's a Wall

where there's a wall
there's a way
around, over, or through
there's a gate
maybe a ladder
a door
a sentinel who
sometimes sleeps
there are secret passwords
you can overhear
there are methods of torture
for extracting clues
to maps of underground passageways
there are zeppelins
helicopters, rockets, bombs
battering rams
armies with trumpets
whose all at once blast
shatters the foundations

where there's a wall
there are words
to whisper by a loose brick
wailing prayers to utter
special codes to tap
birds to carry messages
taped to their feet
there are letters to be written
novels even

on this side of the wall
i am standing staring at the top
lost in clouds
i hear every sound you make
but cannot see you

i incline in the wrong direction
a voice cries faint as in a dream
from the belly
of the wall

from *Woman in the Woods*

Road Building By Pick Axe

1. the highway

driving down the
highway from revelstoke –
the road built by
forced labour – all the
nisei having no
choice etcetera etcetera
and mentioning this in
passing to an englishman
who says when he
came to canada from
england he wanted to
go to vancouver too but
the quota for professors
was full so he was
forced to go to toronto

2. found poem

uazusu shoji
who was twice wounded
while fighting with the princess pats
in world war I
had purchased nineteen acres of land
under the soldiers settlement act
and established a chicken farm

his nineteen acres
a two-storied house
four chicken houses
an electric incubator
and 2,500 fowl
were sold for $1,492.59
after certain deductions

for taxes and sundries were made
mr. shoji received a cheque
for $39.32

   3.   the day after

the day after sato-sensei
received the order of canada
he told some of us nisei
the honour he received
was our honour, our glory
our achievement

and one nisei remembered
the time sensei went to japan
met the emperor
and was given a rice cake
how sensei brought it back to vancouver
took the cake to a baker and
had it crushed into powder
so that each pupil might
receive a tiny bit

and someone suggested
he take the order of canada medal
and grind it to bits
to share with us

   4.   memento

trapped
in a clear plastic
hockey-puck paperweight
is a black ink sketch

of a jaunty outhouse

slocan reunion
august 31, 1974
toronto

   5. may 3, 1981

i'm watching the flapping
green ferry flag on the
way to victoria –
the white dogwood flower
centred by a yellow dot

a small yellow dot
in a b.c. ferry boat –

in the vancouver daily province
a headline today reads
"western canada hatred
due to racism"

ah my british
british columbia my
first brief home

   6. issei in housekeeping room

feeble star rays
leave the surface of her slow turning
hoping to find out there in the night
someone that needs
her needing light
but stars die, she knows

eventually the spinning ends
lights sputter across uninhabited moons
and people who once were needed
no longer are

though she has extinguished
all the beacon candles in her dark
she still flickers –
a small flesh candle
round and round
in her lighthouse

from *Woman in the Woods*

When I Was a Little Girl

when i was a little girl
we used to walk together
tim, my brother who wore glasses
and i, holding hands
tightly as we crossed the bridge
and he'd murmur "you pray now"
– being a clergyman's son –
until the big white boys
had kicked on past –
later we'd climb the bluffs
overhanging the ghost town
and pick the small white lilies
and fling them like bombers
over slocan

from *A Choice of Dreams*

What Do I Remember of the Evacuation

what do i remember of the evacuation?
i remember my father telling tim and me
about the mountains and the train
and the excitement of going on a trip –
what do i remember of the evacuation?
i remember my mother wrapping
a blanket around me and my
pretending to fall asleep so she would be happy
though i was so excited i couldn't sleep
(i hear there were people herded
into the hastings park like cattle –
families were made to move in two hours
abandoning everything, leaving pets
and possessions at gun point –
i hear families were broken up
men were forced to work – i heard
it whispered late at night
that there was suffering) and
i missed my dolls –
what do i remember of the evacuation?
i remember miss foster and miss tucker
who still live in vancouver
and who did what they could
and loved the children and who gave me
a puzzle to play with on the train –
and i remember the mountains and i was
six years old and i swear i saw a giant
gulliver of gulliver's travels scanning the horizon
and when i told my mother she believed it too
and i remember how careful my parents were
not to bruise us with bitterness
and i remember the puzzle of lorraine life
who said "don't insult me" when i
proudly wrote my name in japanese
and tim flew the union jack

when the war was over but lorraine
and her friends spat on us anyway
and i prayed to the god who loves
all the children in his sight
that i might be white

from *A Choice of Dreams*

Snakes

suddenly in the woods a
green and yellow snake as if it
slithered down my back
a moving rope of wind slinking an instant
barber shop sign round my spine
and as i clambered out of the woods –
suddenly on the path a presence
of children, one fearful whispering
"chinese" and the other
moving swiftly past –

from *A Choice of Dreams*

Forest Creatures

on this street there lives a little dark girl
a little dark girl with an orange coat
black stockings and new shiny black shoes
running to school through the mangled forest
one shiny new shoe flung away
by laughing boys with tiger faces –
later my black haired daughter
comes dancing home both shoes on
replying "well she cheats when we play"
but tomorrow they are all together
blue eyes, black hair, orange coat, tiger boys
skipping double dutch in the driveway
colours all blending in a buttery chant

from *A Choice of Dreams*

Woodtick

the spring day the teen on his bike slants his caucasian eyes
at my eight year old beautiful daughter
and taunts gibberish
i am eight years old and the japs are
enemies of canada and the big white boys
and their golden haired sisters who
live in the ghost town of slocan
are walking together, crowding me
off the path of the mountain, me running
into the forest to escape
into the pine brown and green lush dark
and getting lost and fearing woodticks
which burrow into your scalp beneath
thick black hair follicles and can only be
dug out by a doctor with hot needles –
fearing sudden slips caused by melting snow
and steep ravines and the thick silence of
steaming woods and cobwebs, so listening
for the guiding sound of their laughter
to lead me back to the path and
following from a safe distance unseen
till near the foot of the mountain
then running past faster than their laughter
home, vowing never to go again up the mountain
alone – and deidre whispers to walk faster
though i tell her there are no
woodticks in saskatoon

from *A Choice of Dreams*

Calligraphy

my eighty-one year old mother's
penultimate act
before leaving her house
of thirty-one years
was to kill
a large black spider
that stood shock-still
in the bottom
of the bathtub

the calligraphy
lies on the bathtub ledge
a foreign word
of curved spider legs
delicate as brush strokes

from *Woman in the Woods*

July in Coaldale

july in coaldale and
so hot the scalp steams
and i am curling my mother's
fine white hair with her
new mist curler iron
i bought for her
81st birthday and
she is telling me
of her early morning dream
that it was christmas and
there was music – "i can't
remember the song" she says
but after a few more curls
she is singing in japanese
"joy to the world"
somewhat out of tune
because she is deaf now
and her throat is dry but
she was famous for her
singing once and
she says in her dream
there was an old dry plant
that started to bloom

from *Woman in the Woods*

Leaving Her Waving At The Airport

i am reminded of the three
red frozen apples on her
leafless december tree
which she said would gradually
disintegrate or disappear

small and wrinkled and
hanging in there till perhaps
the next snowstorm

from *Jericho Road*

Coaldale Poem

in the heat of summer
coaldale is full
of blue bottle flies
rasping at the windows –
small print gossipers
petitpoint buzzards

coaldale dear coaldale
your dot and tittle preachers
your black winged puritans
tell me how i may not live
or write of love

since what i've written
is forbidden i take
the small pink eraser
on the end of my pencil
the flesh of it
soft on my lip
flesh erasing flesh

gem of the west
i remember you
town of the fly swatter
town of the uncaressed

from *Woman in the Woods*

She Has Been Here For Three Months

she has been here for three months
silent as a saint on trial and
regal as a snow queen – sometimes
with a sudden smiling grace a
child's face, she moves through the
nursing home thick with
stammering woodpeckers in her
private popcorn tree country

gone from her familiar orchard
to a glacial whiteness she picks
with great delicacy the fruits
of her new winter trees

daily she waits for her
grandchild's letters –
sometimes on walker
sometimes in wheelchair
she breathes the country odour
of last fall's hay
and watches the dandelions
growing white

and whiter and blowing finally
tiny umbrella puffs
across the open field
and everywhere she sees
the earth bled to stubble
dry husks of hay
dry egg shells

it is time, dry time
all crying past
it is time burning
burning in the air

and the small white
dandelion seedlings
are smoke trails showing
the pathway home

from *Woman in the Woods*

Stations of Angels

within the universe of flame
in the time between
watching and waiting
are the fire creatures
holy and unholy
hungry for those
many coloured parts of us
which have no names

blow out the candle, friends
quickly, and let us
close our eyes
while the devouring
is at hand

at the heart of our stillness, in
peaceable flames we shall
hear
shall we not hear
our mothers
singing?

from *Woman in the Woods*

Small Rock

they didn't know it was a small rock
in the middle of the road
caused the bike to swerve
and hit the ditch
what was real was his being
smashed open and ambulances wailing
and everyone weeping --
the little lie was never blamed

Old Man in the Library

old now and
nameless for me this
man in the library

like a beheaded flower
he blooms here briefly
in my mind's bowl
his stems leaves roots
elsewhere in a room perhaps
nearby

fingers of both hands
cut to the knuckles
he adjusts his glasses
smooths the newspaper
opens and closes his mouth
making short clucking sounds

patiently slowly he
tries several times to
turn the page

from *Jericho Road*

In The Forest

in the forest the tree
perfectly balances its hours
in the time of its branches
no branch is accidental

in the forest our arms
perfectly balance the breeze
in the time of our departures
no leaving is accidental

in autumn
in the bare room
by a crack in the window
a curtain moves

as the woodsman arrives
precisely beyond time

from *Woman in the Woods*

For David

not as we dreamed or planned
did life fling us
nor by thought's search
did we find our way
but by walking
were our limbs discovered
and the pathway formed
chance and change
not of our choosing
uncovered what we decided

from *Woman in the Woods*

Communication

you
are swathed
in layers of silly chains
which i may not cut
or burn or wrench away from you
because you love them
to reach you
i must first say
'how beautiful are your chains today'
then i must kneel
and tap my message on your chains
and hope
that you will hear

from *The Splintered Moon*

Yet There Was Bathsheba

thinking about this holy matrimony thing
and old king david taking sacred food
from the temple to give his starving men
like we love-starved, life-hungry
marriage-broken warriors seeking
sacred love in holy places – our
inner heart of hearts tearing the veils
of lovers, counselors, psychiatrists, whores
or who have you – feasting gingerly
beneath the cherubim while outside
rage philistine doubts and guilts reminding us
that king david another time when thirsty
threw away the dearly won water
his men brought him, making
no game of his thirst and daring
to risk no life for love –
(yet there was bathsheba
and all david's guilt triumphant
couldn't keep wisdom from issuing forth
from that unholy bond)

from *Jericho Road*

Therapist

he walks into the sphere with his
invisible mile-long shield
flattening people into
one-dimensional slabs on which
he draws his graphs and charts
carefully avoiding the use of any
four-letter words

he is charles atlas holding up
a flat-circle world and
talking to his audience in
balloon-enclosed messages

we are serious as children
with comic books we
believe in superman

from *Jericho Road*

Garden Poem

"marigolds" he said
rooting her firmly
in his garden bed
"are sacrificial plants
for garden slugs"

she wiped the telling slime
from red-rimmed eyes
grew dragon leaves at dusk
turned dandelion

and in every neat
suburban lawn
she nestled her tiny
umbrellas down

from *Woman in the Woods*

Plastic Yellow Rose Beneath the Piano

the way the flower grew
was not to her liking
she poked it impatiently
nipped it, drowned it out
left it withering for years
thinking perhaps some miraculous bloom
would suddenly burst out
or hoping it might disappear
decay or dry and blow away
but it survived secretly
in its dusty hours
did not die
nor grow nor open
an amazing endurance
and patience which neither
blooms nor fades love is
patient they say

from *Jericho Road*

Leaf

this which once clung
to tree branch
which with cold and colder
wind was flung

this our leaving
rain trapped and brown
as earth and dung
soiled our walk

with rake and plastic
garbage bag with
new coat and haircut
we buried the fall

from *Jericho Road*

For Gordon at Seven

what an extremist he was
nebuchadnezzar
always threatening to
kill off people – by
sword by fire and
limb from limb

in this suburb lives a
small daniel daring and
daring to worship no
gods of mine and heaven help him
daily he saunters off
among wild beasts in
dungeons of my creating
yet daily he is back safely
o praise the god of small
extremist here whose
name may be daniel or
nebuchadnezzar, i
don't really know who he is
or whom i am in relation to him
but somehow we are both here
everyday testing testing
1, 2, 3, 4, testing, are you
there god?

from *Woman in the Woods*

Grief Poem

o that after all no
thought breaks
the mind's cold spell

chilled
these bones their
language lost

in this fesh silence
weather hides all
odours of decay

by freezing time
i travel through
this numb day

look look
my small
my beautiful child

the icicle here
how it shimmers
in the blue sun

my small
my beautiful child
look once more
into the shimmering

from *Woman in the Woods*

Bird Poem

when deidre was so angry she
could only droop with it after
hitting the wall so hard she said
her hand was broken and i
could hardly remember that much
helplessness and rage

i am prepared for many forms
of farewell, but this? a
bandaged wing, a wild bird
my fifteen-year-old high school girl

i wait without push or pull
through rage and flight and
unexpected landings
as did my mother with her
long-distance night praying
her cage of arms
a net and nest

from *Jericho Road*

To Scuttle the Moon

wandering, august evening, down the mall
to the lights spawning in the canal
a thousand low-slung baby moons
and fisherfolk groggy with bait
looking with lunar hooks
for late-night sea creatures

comes a man offering
cigarettes, conversation, a fishy stare
then – great immortal whale day –
he slops into her lap, a
tidal wave of blubbering –
is this a fisherman's reward?

she flounders from the taffy pull
to scuttle the moon and the sailing swans

from *Jericho Road*

No Worms on Her Hook

there are no worms on her hook
no bait on her line
she is inexpert
in catching fish
the sea is the sound of her needing
the fish her objects of love
and she has no taste for seafood
somewhere in the vague distance
cormorants fly
pursuing the teeming sea
she trusted the moon to glow for a spell
and show her the living waters
but there is only a rippling
and the moon is a splintered shell
she trusts the splintered moon
to keep her from drifting too close
to the deadly shore
to keep her eyes from seeing too much
of hungry birds

from *The Splintered Moon*

Tulip Centerpiece

in the restaurant
a small gang of
smoking swearing
pre-teen girls
clumped together as if
they'd been planted
in the middle of a
highway and ordered to
grow and each one
tough and surviving
like the pink plastic
tulip centerpiece they're
using for an ashtray

from *Jericho Road*

Grey Lady

within the new glass walled office
the grey lady crept
with her scrub bucket and her mop
scouring the scars
the black heel skuff marks of the man
against the pockety pock dents
of the high heels
the scrub lady toiled
on hardened knees, leather encased hands
her own soft moccasined feet
leaving no mark on the floor

Moon Walk

take care in the night travellings
walk into traffic with light feet
the moon's highways are crowded
the sky full of dust

walk gently in the night crossings
your side of the street has the short cuts
in the end you will come
to the spot where you first met

the police are not watching
and jay walking meets no disapproval
but walk carefully, the streets are wide
and traffic thick as on earth's freeways

from *Woman in the Woods*

Hitchhiker

cars streaking past
and he says there are trees as well as cars
pain and benediction, parting
and meeting again
and that to believe otherwise
is to be a worshipper of cars
is to be a small animal sacrifice
on a busy highway

from *Jericho Road*

Stutterer

he kept stumbling off the polished world
silent with sandy tongue
at introductions
all his witty missiles
internally doused
"all children's veins should be cut at birth
because those who survive
will be stronger for having undergone the test"
she said slithering away
her tongue slicing the air
while he stammered and bled

from *Jericho Road*

It Dies by Detour

the honeybee slaps crazily
against the bus window
its intricate map dancing
journey between nectar and hive
scrambled against the
transparent wall

from *Woman in the Woods*

Train Trip

sitting beside the strange
man on the train, she
hangs her coat over his
the hood covering
his brown collar the
blue arm bumping
bumping against
the brown elbow patch

intimate
the clothes caress
in the rock rock of the train
while discarded on the seat
they travel together
polite as death

from *Woman in the Woods*

Like Spearing a Butterfly

like spearing a butterfly
me in my dream
dead with a sword in my belly
the villagers scattering

night falls in
drops of flesh from a
rotting sun

a million hair-thin
spider legs leap from her skull
skeletal as wind
she approaches

without a word
she watches
her eyes grow fat

from *Jericho Road*

Greeting My Father

i can hardly remember
the last time i wore heels
clack clack clackity clack
on the marble floor
at the bus station
assert assert assert
yes this is how it was
in the arrogant hair bouncing days
before failure

father i have come to greet you
wearing a mid-calf skirt
twelve guests will be coming
for dinner in your honour
at my ex-husband's luxury apartment

isn't it almost, father,
as you would have wished

from *Woman in the Woods*

Biting Silences

the neat way they eat
indicates nobility
but occasionally
they dine with pack rats
fangs at the table are fine
sometimes

afterwards, they burn my letters
in the fireplace

from *A Choice of Dreams*

Bread For Sale

there's this no-good typewriter
on this ridiculously high narrow plant stand
in front of the store on a slanted hill
and no matter how you try
flicking the ribbon lever from white to black
to red and pound and back-space
the word "understand" won't come through
there's this typewriter sliding off
the plant stand and all the messed-up
papers mushing up the gears
and the invisible word punched on
and the whole heave-ho dropping
like dung down a huge hole
full of staring people –
and all the time the man in the store
lines his shelves with fresh bread

from *Jericho Road*

Snake Dance

a semantic dance, the
politeness pulses along
scales slippery with speech

from the slow long dwarf star centre
gravitational pull of
submerged need the
body's coils recoil on
the skin of our lies

we smile the theatrical
smiles that mask our
moving, our minds are
almost mesmerized
into belief

from *Jericho Road*

Three Dreams

1
i rub the toy train on my sleeve
dusting it carefully
moving its wheels etcetera
wondering where the motor is
where the genie is

2
on board the ship we find there are
many ways to cut the apple
to make the exquisite tiny ridges
for a special apple dessert
it's the sort of thing that belongs
in a world without wars

3
she looks out the window
seeing the fire of the wars coming
we rush outside to rid ourselves of poison
we vomit profusely and make dung mounds
and this is our sole preparation

the day of lies approaches
if we tell all before the enemy comes
he will find the village emptied
and only the wind in the temple left
waiting to do him battle

how shall i tell of apples
in a world of wars

from *A Choice of Dreams*

Minerals from Stone

for many years
androgynous with truth
i molded fact and fantasy
and where they met
made the crossroads home

here the house built
by lunatic limbs
fashioning what is not
into what might be

a palace cave
for savage saints with
hunting knife still moist

bring me no longer
your spoils, my lioness
i have a house in the
shadows now and have
learned to eat minerals
straight from stone

from *Woman in the Woods*

Bread to Stone

turned to stone
she asked for bread
they offered cakes
and as she waited
the food
within her grasp
turned to stone
she asked for bread

from *Jericho Road*

She Is Wanted

time unwinds his limbs
his sarcophagus bindings
his catatonic eyes re-adjust
he rises stiff as death

he steps into his van
'to serve and to protect'
he cruises the alleys
with searchlight and siren
and his many unknown weapons

she is wanted
dead or alive

blood drops on the rock pile
slowly sucking the stone
the red juice grows grey and granular

he asks her to sign
on the dotted line
beside the official seal
red and jagged as a saw blade

from *Jericho Road*

Pray My Mantis

dread this daily
mourning news

pray my lord mantis
it is not so
our green limbs an instant
and the screeching birds over all

from *A Choice of Dreams*

Certain Ants

certain ants
in seasons of rain
cluster together
into ant balls
that tumble over
troubled waters
till they touch
dry land

in this season
of much drowning
much clutching
and clustering
it is enough
to breathe
occasionally

from *Woman in the Woods*

Here We Are a Point of Sanity

here we are a point of sanity
while cars are leaping
over the edges of mountain cliffs
and someone broadcasts that the victims
will be lucky if they live
and there's a sky full of smoke from the wreck
and we're holding a hose and shooting water out
from way up here on top of a mountain

for what? for what?

what we need are people on the scene –
healing people crazy people
people with seven league boots
and ready arms to
carry the rage – what we need
are shovels and axes and
mad mad friends
to plunge to the bottom
unafraid

oh leap down leap down
to the thirst
to the flame

from *Woman in the Woods*

The Girl Who Cried Wolf

"i love you" she said
"i do not lie"
she showed him the slash in her arm
"how can you sit there" she asked
"just sit there sit there"
"because" he said "it is the way of wolves"

from *A Choice of Dreams*

Open Marriage

walking at night under the
intermittent street lights
their shadows fade and grow
back to front, short to long
weightless patches of grey
over the skittering snow

like peter pan they are
in search of their shadows and
constantly checking, these
freedom-heavy days

from *Jericho Road*

Transplant

it's a matter of being
uprooted by this gardener secretly
in the long dark night of my
growing and planted in the
sudden noon day trembling
green house touch of his
hands – it's a matter of blossoms
exploding through the roots of my
slow black hair and being
trapped by the tendrils

from *A Choice of Dreams*

Erasure

the night i sleep in his house
i have a nightmare about a
tiny blue eraser baby boy i
want desperately to save but
finally i am weeping and
asking if after all it is
maybe ethically and morally
right to abort

i waken and hear him
sleeping nearby – how much
i wonder, do we choose to die?
i rub the dreaming from the day
cover the mind's embers
with waking

from *Jericho Road*

Flowering

the whole approach seems
too young somehow
i mean – not because
nudity is offensive, indeed
there is a glory in bronze
but i resent your insistence
that all must be tested
by the fire of our hot eyes –
love flowers
when we deal gently
with shadows

from *A Choice of Dreams*

Note to a Gentleman

the time
to talk about your wife
is before

it is the difference
between a shield
and a sword

and if you want the battle
to be fought without arms
bring her with you

from *Woman in the Woods*

If Your Mirror Breaks

if when you are holding a
hand mirror while sitting
in the front seat of a car
and the mirror breaks
you must stop everything quickly
step on the brakes
leap from the car

if when you are holding in
your arms a mirror and you
feel the glass sudden in your veins
if your throat bleeds with
brittle words and you
hear in the distance the
ambulance siren

if your mirror breaks into a
tittering sound of tinkling glass
and you see the highway stretch
into a million staring splinters
you must stop everything gently
wait for seven long years
under a sky of whirling wheels

if your mirror breaks
oh if your mirror breaks

from *Woman in the Woods*

On the Jericho Road

your tongue
was your weapon
i lay silent
on the jericho road

silence is also
a two-edged sword

these words
are my donkey

from *Jericho Road*

Tonight Notice

a butterfly
emerging from its cocoon
voluntarily without prodding
the upside down brown sky
branch of its emerging
dropping away as wings
walk the air

yesterday the bullet questions

tonight, notice
the armoured butterfly
plowing the brown sky

from *Jericho Road*

Strange Green Shoot

strange green shoot in this
middle-aged garden is it
weed? is it vegetable? does she
pull it out now or wait
to see what it might be –
she grows more curious
than executive

every minute its
roots descend through
skull through throat
leafing underground foliage

too late for uprooting
but there's scissor in hand
bleeding to dust
that thin green thing

mistress wary and contrary
how does these days
the garden grow?

with dust and ash
with ash and dust
and fine white fragile bones

from *Woman in the Woods*

The Aquarium Has Its Own Silences

feeling your letter this morning
while staring in the aquarium
colourful male guppies and
fat grey mother with babies which
cling to the camouflage of greens

and remembering that chunky woman of my childhood
her short bow legs and sturdy walk
her endless procession of children
and her handsome quiet husband
committing adultery with his secretary
the village rocking with gossip
when their baby bulged the secretary dress

and the chunky woman left her brood one day
kerchief on, churning her legs, seeking
the edge of the village with her darting eyes –
i stared and stared the way
i stare this morning at these fish

your words dart among the pebbles
in the confines of my mind. i close
my eyes for love of newborn guppies
and flounder silently, the village
heavy in my veins

from *Jericho Road*

Walk In Aquarium

after our heavy talk we walk
to the aquarium and see in one tank
soft blue velvet fish yellow
srtiped ones with foxy faces
succulent sea cucumbers – and
beside this display, a sample
of current harbour waters with
crabs, some starfish, flounders,
a coke can covered in brown sline

after heavy talks it is not
always easy to forgive, the
words cling, unresolved debris
rests in waiting pools – it is
not always easy to remember
there are other ways to speak
deeper waters safer
than this harbour

from *Jericho Road*

Wild Rose Bush

in the middle of our constant
penultimate argument he
went to the wild thorny bush
in the tame garden to
pick the rose, tugging and twisting but
finally, leaving it there he returned
and sat beside me, coughing softly while
the bent branch of the injured bush
moved with imperceptible grace
in the elastic afternoon

from *Jericho Road*

Street Walking

walking through the locked-up suburb
every locked door, part of a tunnel wall
every locked door, a denial of a resting place
the coach suggests her calves are developing
the calluses on her feet are
excellent for treading coals
he suggests she will be grateful
when she wins an endurance medal
she tells him he can have the medals
they are too heavy and
clank in the dark

from *Woman in the Woods*

It Wouldn't Be So Bad

if i were a brown cow on the prairie
by a water hole, lying on
thistles under the sun
never having lain on a double
mattress in an air-conditioned
apartment – if i were, i say,
a brown cow, placidly swishing
flies off my rump –

and if you were a crow
on a telephone post
having chosen of all the
miles of posts that
particular one without
days of indecision –

and you were to flap away
when the truck came roaring
down the highway

from *Jericho Road*

October 3

we were watching the ducks
in the middle of the river
the current swift as our blood
and the ducks
looking as if they were
not moving at all

we were as if
standing still watching the ducks
and he said
"should we fly south"

i said "yes"
and he talked about other things
while i stared at
the idiotic ducks

later there were
no ducks later
still no
river

from *A Choice of Dreams*

She Sends Old Photographs

i take the pictures
but not with match and flame
with fingertips and bandages
digging with careful fingernails
i peel the crackling memories
from his skin

brown as antique blood
brown as old frost on
dirty windows, i wipe the
dark stains from his eyes
my lips are red with rust

from *Jericho Road*

Washday

how can the wash get clean
if the water is not clear
if there are buckets of mud
in the washing machine

it is true, after awhile
the mud becomes very clean
after awhile the scream
thins into silence, the corpse
turns to air after awhile

already straw bodies
are wind-frayed
the heart pumps
clots of air
spasms of mud

time will change all this
the sheets will blow in the sunny weather
someone else will fold them

from *Jericho Road*

We Were Talking About Stability

finally all the deceptions –
cloud, flight, departure
and i have said i do not
trust anymore but what
do i believe on this
plane? above? these clouds?
we are, i know, walking
on meringues and broken
egg shells, aren't we
and trampling it all
solid

from *A Choice of Dreams*

Parting Shots

he is sitting in a puddle
of hairs there in a
forest of bulrushes and
swampland trees he is
sitting watching the small
kingfisher bird and the twig
and the blue he is watching
all the land around
morning moving slow as
sleep and snail even the
flight of birds is caught
on film and still as a
cat's startled stare he sees
the falling bird its
one wing lifted forever
as it salutes the earth and
here the rifle and waterproof boots
and there the camera and
click – the latch – click
the tiny language of
terror don't
go please she
says without at least
breakfast

from *Woman in the Woods*

The Signs Were Everywhere

she was a fast-dancing
laughing leaping willow lady
an evening's delight – the signs
were everywhere and they were
eager then to go half-naked
and half-crazed into the night

now their touch is parched
as prairie, the sandstorms
blow over sun-baked skin
they did not know that moon
creatures sleep at noon and
lunar signs reverse their shadows
through every revolution of light

from *Jericho Road*

And You Talk and Talk

walking barefoot through spring forest
mud, tangle brush and mottled leaf
feet plastered with messages and
being barefoot in a warm forest
love words are compulsory
predictable as a tv serial

it is as if we have stepped
into an icy stream, the winter water
searing the clinging brown and revealing
a red cut trickling across our
leather boots

from *Jericho Road*

Finally That There Is

no corner left in which to hide
the mouse, the cat
the empty room
the one defense left
is not to move at all
not to write
not to think
not to send you this letter

finally in the cat's jaws
i remember the secret door
listen for your tunneling
realize finally that
you are the cat
you are the mouse
you are the room without doors
you are the secret tunnel

finally this fatal defense
fangs sharp with belief
back arched and clawing
the heart's walls

from *A Choice of Dreams*

To Wash Away the Green

before she said "goodbye forever"
he took a pretend paint brush
dipped it in a bucket of green
and painted magic circles
muttering "paint paint" as he walked
round and round with incantations
he flipped drops of tart
green grapes on the floor

when she said "goodbye forever"
the children snatched the pretend brush
dipped it in a purple pot
and painted distant mountains
one colour sunsets, purple roses
in a goodbye sky – they strung a curtain
of purple grapes and shed plump purple tears

from *Woman in the Woods*

She Has Fled

she (the wife
the nameless one)
has fled
to where the
name tree grows
its leaves
in the breezes
rustling

and he
stripped bare
sits where she
sat before

his arms
grown moist
as snail's eyes
search
the sky where
two small kites
are flying

seeking
strings

from *Woman in the Woods*

Afterwards

after he took
the budgie to the vet
and a needle pierced
its thin feathered belly
and it died
its arthritic claws clutching
nothing –

after he
cleaned the cage
and threw out the
leftover seeds and gravel
after he made the room
clean and neat –

what remained in his mind
was the budgie's grey claw
unnaturally straight
and his small daughter's
forefinger curved
stroking the tiny head

from *Woman in the Woods*

Wind Poem

when the window is open
and the night enters
blinds flap
branches scratch the roof
the candle is blown out

we pull the blanket higher
our hungry fingertips
pick berries in the moonlight

and there are no mosquitoes
or blackflies
because the wind is blowing

from *Woman in the Woods*

We Did Not Ask

leaving the shine and clank
of metal ship for the
vine-entangled raft and
drifting downstream back
to the long prowling night
of leopards, lynxes, reptiles
in the dark

when we set out on our
explorations bravely over the
black waters we intended no
wrecked ship creaking on the rocks

strange this unmapped land
the street lights spit and disappear
lightning cracks, stiffened cats
crouch in the bushes, children flee

we call and call the
wilderness peers through our
glowing eyes we did not
ask for terror we did not
seek this transformation

from *Jericho Road*

The Morning She Leaves

the morning she leaves
the sky is the colour
of the charcoal blue pigeons
that strut on the roof next door
and an endless double row
of curly branched winter trees
submit to the pruner's sheers

the morning she leaves
the sky is thrashing
with dark pigeon wings
and dead branches
are gathered like hay

from *Woman in the Woods*

Bast, the Cat Goddess

the spirit of the cat goddess
stalks her walk through the
halls of the british museum
pouncing at her eyes
a sleek black icon
lower Egyptian diety

an inaudible yowl
thin and commanding as a
magnetic beam pierces
the glass case

it is for this, for this
for this you are made, to
pulse, to spring, to move
in an unapologetic dream

the hairs on her body
rise like iron filings

from *Jericho Road*

Raphael's "The Miraculous Draught of Fishes"

in london's victoria and albert museum
christ sits miraculously with two
full grown men in a
boat tinier than a bathtub

his white robe
reflects in the water
red as a sunset
red as a pool of blood

the sign says "the robe was
painted in a mixture of white
and a fugitive pink lake pigment
out of which the latter has faded
in the reflection the robe
was painted in vermilion
a permanent red pigment"

a trinity of black birds
flamingo-like creatures
tread the water's edge

from *Jericho Road*

Experiment

first a series of
tamed and tamable rodents
raised in cages with
mazes, food pellets, electric
shocks, gloved hands

next a wild rat
fresh from foraging through
wheat fields, rain storms
dodging predators with
brilliance with wizardry
a warrior of the woodlands
a general bearing scars

the researcher reports on
helplessness in animals
he says the wild rat swam
for sixty hours
before it drowned

he publishes his article
in *psychology today*
and makes an addition
to his curriculum vitae

from *Woman in the Woods*

Day One at the PMO

initially one is aware
of the odour of fur
of the hints of flesh
on the bared incisors

one notes the carefully arranged
surgeon's tools
on this reverse
island of dr. moreau

a chair with arms
a chair without arms
a carpet
a door
a window, two windows
a phone with buttons
a phone without buttons

initially one is aware
of scufflings in the corridors
one views the new
appearance of one's limbs
with alarm
initially

from *Jericho Road*

Office Toad

fat, hop-heavy
and bulbous-eyed
watching for one
fluttering step

our limbs leap-ready
risk no closeness

one kiss my swift
amphibious prince your
lasso lips your
glue-tipped tongue

toads, yes
but not for kissing

from *Jericho Road*

The Success Ladder

with each rung we
ascend deeper into
our bowels we become
tortuous as intestines

we cling with our
signatures and our
cunning friendliness
we climb on the
labour of others

at the grinning end
at the slippery top
waits the hungry
serpent we worship

it spreads a table
before us in the
presence of our
enemies it
feasts on us forever
its cups overflows

from *Jericho Road*

Elitism

is a cumin seed
you place between
your teeth – its
shell as intact
as unhusked wild rice

bite
and the sudden
release of flavour
is a tiny assault
in your mouth

the husk falls free
and departs
to its husk heave

meanwhile
the rest of the meal
bows to cumin

cumin bread
cumin salad
cumin curry

from *Woman in the Woods*

"chrises"

sleeping crumpled bag
in urine soaked city
stairwell concrete corner
and black word
scrawled large
on streaky wall

CHRISES

christ
we are in crisis
no place to
urinate or defecate

every night you
rest in pieces
rags and rages
and contra
dictions

Offerings

what you offer us –
a soap bubble
a glass thread –
what you place
in our open hands
one branch of
one snow fleck
a sliver of smoke

and if and if
the offering bursts
breaks
melts
if the smoke
is swallowed in the night

we lift
the barricades
we take the edges
of our transience
we bury the ashes
of our absences
and sift
the silences

from *Woman in the Woods*

For A Blank Book

i have peculiar
leaf shaped ears
my fur is
forest coloured

when your flesh
first uttered words
i lost understanding

you said i attend
stone and not flesh
source and not blood
bread and not bone

your flesh
your blood
your bone

which brings you to
mistrust of me

and all the while
the stone bleeds
the source calls your name
the bread is broken

but you cannot see
or hear
or taste

listen then, my love
to the wind blowing
and the sound of breath
over the grassy forest floor

but know i did not bend
to the right or to the left
all the while
that i loved you

from *Woman in the Woods*

For Ben and Malcolm

i have come to the
united jewish appeal
with the slogan "we are one"
tattooed on my timid gentile heart
wearing my "why not" button on my
blue winter park, announcing
the east and other categories

i am sitting at our
table of differences
declaring the slogan
to all who come

listen!
the sounds of fingernails
under the table
are sharp as the teeth of mice

forgive me
i am obsessed with history
and always scratching for clues

from *Woman in the Woods*

Last Day

that day walking to work
the last day of the world
seeing everything for the last time
the sidewalk café empty
a cabbie sleeping in his seat
office workers walking in the wind
everyone conspiring
to make the last day
as normal as every other
the air swished up through the vent
making the calendar dance on the wall
the riveters on the building next door
continued to break concrete
the stenos clacked the typewriter keys
the women in the hall
talked about their babies

that day walking to work
the sun low on the horizon
red and huge, an erratic sunset
everyone decided not to notice
not to stare
and in the elevator
no-one tried to be
unusually friendly

from *Woman in the Woods*

In the Almost Evening

in the almost evening loneliest time of day
i looked out the window and could see sky
and i said "sky, what can you give me?"
and sky said, "i can give you sunset" so i
looked at sunset with moon and star
and said "sunset what can you give me?"
and sunset said "we can give you skyline"
and i looked at skyline with bright lights
and i said "what can you give me" and
skyline said "we'll give you people" and
i said to people, "people give me love"
and people said "too busy"
so in the almost evening loneliest time of day
i took to listening feverishly

from *Jericho Road*

Breezes

the weeping willow sways low
in the breeze it seems to brush
the tops of those distant bushes
sensuously in my one dimensional
perception – once i imagined
i knew so well the meaning
of your careful words brushing
my mind gently with a nearness
now i see how distant
the bushes are i still
would paint them touching

from *A Choice of Dreams*

Rooster

spear or smirk what does it matter
what the weapon is the wounds
need tending need tenderness
what does it matter where the
error lies
these days i
hear the rooster calling
its feet rooted in the night
its wings in the morning this is
still the time
to forgive, to be forgiven

from *A Choice of Dreams*

Forgiveness

the fruit takes from the sun
the skin swells thin green
to red to ripeness
until the time for giving
when the wind
thuds and seeds the earth
and the rich brown soil
receives the flight down

and to walk at that moment
in the orchard again
when the children
are still small
and to see
in the sunlight
how the blossoms are falling

from *Woman in the Woods*

Trilliums

sudden in late
april forest floor
white trilliums
bright epitaphs
brief memories of winter

last december
the sun no longer
melted the snow
snowflakes fell
in the glittering air

with flattering words
futile promises
with such devices and
conspiracies of ice
the winds erected a tomb

but from below
in ontario, always
in spring time
trilliums

from *Woman in the Woods*

Water Garden

All The Trees Coloured Were

all the trees coloured were
bird full and song ready to move
the forests alive with leaf swish and
ballet shoes on when suddenly
the 'no' storm fell cloud down
and curtain heavy i
cocoon the dark
         grope
my fingernails black
the strange –
everywhere the strange
no colours left –

from *A Choice of Dreams*

Dear Euclyd

moon announces at the end of my dream
"dear euclyd
i am indestructible
i am star"

july thursday 1971 new york
from the airplane we drop
ant powder on entire continents of bloodless ants
like rain on dolly's parade
the ticker tape confetti turning ash white
it's just a matter of time now
the cars crawling like paramecia
in drying drops

9:40 sleepwalk into hot muggy new york
stew people leaping from pot to pot
swim through stop lights computer talk
please detach and retain this stub
for your personal use detach please
your personal stub and retain your use
do not fold staple or mutilate
give name age serial number
ride up elevator – salute – all that is
tinier than tom thumb is not human
it is written on the screen of our understanding
east side clinic 11:00 a.m.

i had the choice – the dreamer has
a choice of dreams – i have
the choice still to turn about
in this tight tunnel ant corridor
carrying my huge white ant egg
with all these other worker ants
our antennae flashing urgency the choice

is still ours what are we
doing here, toby, sandra
hiding from what menace sharing our
microscopic nightmare offering these
cells these souls these bodies to be a
reasonable holy and living sacrifice
to whom for what?

strange what surroundings we regret –
that non-passionate june night
briefly your shadow leapt through
the dark red channel of pre-birth
exploded star bright into incandescent life
palpitated in a cosmos alive with expectation
for how many days did you
grow wildly hopeful until your heart
barely beating in an entirely new sky
died. black. my star child. i would
wish for you another age, another mother

once did god
flood away an imperfect creation
and now the imperfection remains
and an ark full of regret
my small noah, it is to another world
you must go, not the
vacuum aspirator fast drying world
i walk on daily not this
morning and evening time heavy
gasping to find laughter this
dark mist stumbling i
am inuit mother pursed by starving
beasts and howling blizzard
and i abandon you here, here in the

white numbing coldness, your face i dare not
look at for an instant longer you are
dead before you are alive and i don't know how
my limbs move when it is i
should lie there with you the foreign judge
proclaiming my guilt and calling me
murderer but my legs only frostbitten
move on stumbling in the perpetual winter
farther and farther always now to
silences i seek the silences how did
all this happen where did this
come from this wild strange city
this long night of strange people
strangers strangers strangers
jungle creatures talking
jungle talk there is
no escape only this secret scurrying
i understand henceforth every
cockroach approach the
scuttling disappearing i am
familiar with the world of spray
with swatters what escape in this
buzzing of flies in these
patterns the air creates for them
buzz buzz buzz there is
dance of web spider flea there is
a crack in which i crouch
conspicuous in my craving for a
cloak of invisibility i am imprisoned by
the eyes the stars within and without
the constellations i reached and denied
with the denial by which i am denied

i am cut off i have
trampled a universe i have
transgressed the law of holiness
i have eaten the blood
it is *my* blood
is it not my blood?
those watery red tissues in glass bottle
bits of debris, flotsam, fish skin
is this my child drowning in a
fiery sea this sudden tidal wave
this rush of mud over pompeii
can you hear the rushing child, this world
is not for you, nor you not yet, for it
nor i, we are dust, lint, speck, food for
vacuum cleaners we are blood together
in a maelstrom of leviticus we are
flushed out of caves in moreau's island

baby baby it is finished now
but stay with me stay in this
perfect world let me keep you
alive let me hold your warm
body let me baby keep you
from the arguments this time the
newspapers it's a friendly woods we
walk in on grass as soft as quilts
we are together in this deep soft trap
this well this long falling i
tripped the latch with my own hand
i have not stumbled i have rushed
headlong towards the breakers
carrying you tossing you from cliffs
i have burnt you on many altars

offered you to the village elders
for their evening meals, my ram-child
my isaac without a saving god –

it is my faith that died
long before you were conceived
and my ice covered legs move more
slowly now it is the love law
we must yet obey and how have i loved you?

euclid was it child of your spirit
hovering round my moon hollowed night
is it your ears i have deafened
and your dead universe now
in which i pray? the books tell us
the place of your birth is uncertain
i confess i could not have stood
your craving for perfection
where did you go so quickly were you so
uninsistent on life you died so easily
could you not have fought a little at the oven door
performed a mere daniel in a den
could you not convince me or this
italian doctor my accomplice your
father my accomplice could you not through
the long wrestling night of excuses and lies
shout down the executioner with his
'life must die that life might live'
was it you euclid, arguing with the moon?
do you weight me now?

the tides do not return the beaches
fill with harpooned whales
cupid as harpoon king grows weary

and sleeps amid poisoned spears
jonah lies rotting in the store-room
nineveh is lost – you were
a small fish struggling for three minutes
on the prongs of a well aimed hook
are you somewhere now euclyd?
was your angel not yet assigned:
did we throw you back?

i swam upstream and discovered
the river was an eddy in a larger stream
the choices were ripples in a waterfall
the ripples fell like niagara
how many stars drowned today
how many possibilities have been denied

my dream daemon leaves my night watching
but the waiting will return to the silences
the rainbow was a promise of fire
but new signs follow
there are patterns more hidden than our patterning
deaths more lasting than our murderings
there are celebrations still in the surety of death
and more resurrections than i have known

friday july 71 ottawa
"dear euclyd" the dead moon has announced
"i am indestructible
i am star"

from *A Choice of Dreams*

Snowdrift

how the sun defines it
the snow blowing up
thin as a shadow
tiny rockets of glare dust
forming a sharp drift bank
the wind carving a knife of sun drops

behind our half-closed eyes
the moon turns slowly
gathering the shape

from *Jericho Road*

Waiting Room

midnight and the monks
move down the corridor
"dona nobis pacem"
the elves in the forest
the leaves breathing
doctors, nurses
white in the moonlight –
beneath a toppled toadstool
clusters of ants carry white eggs
struggle through collapsing tunnels

from *A Choice of Dreams*

Poem for Wednesday
   (for John)

winter, 1971, ottawa

the report comes by
voice or pen, by telephone, by
letter or lack of letter

the calendar flaps tick pat
tick pat on white walls
air vent whooshing a
steady metallic endless
november of nurses, doctors
porcelain people frozen in
edgy groupings around his bed
his body taut as a bent bow
eyes leaping like arrows
across the battleground between
winter and hope with winter
winning the anaesthetist watching
the weakening pulse

beneath the ice the lake
is an endless wound festering with
prehistoric murk, he sits in a
garden of anchors resplendent with
small darting shrimp colourless
in the depths, wife, children,
friends, mother, praying in the
ice-locked ark their patterned
dreams weighting the ends of
his buried rainbow and swirling
like coloured eels in the
swarming dark

i remember we were tender we
were tentative as lightning lost
in the dance of northern skies, no
word spoken no touch no greeting
or farewell, suspended in
the mind's landscape, the
morning's sun broom sweeping away
our footprints in the melting drifts

is it enough that we once
luminous yellow and green after rain
met secret elm, secret willow, each
tree breeze-shaped, our leaves
riotous with light, the brief hour
edged with sparrows grey and flitting
the tree roots unsprung along the
banks our hands leaping up the
sky's stairs the vines of our minds
branching in pinpoint strands of
touch and spring fireflies is it
enough?

i sit in the night garden dark
auditorium with questing hands
in the attitude of trees
asking

what strange trick was this, lord
that you stood us a moment in eden
cut off our hands and commanded us
to eat that you command us now to
walk in a sudden water garden
without feet what strange trick
is this?

listening here at the edge of
king solomon's courtyard in the
cloud of accusing rain, my tongue
a knife in the smothering crowd i
do not know king solomon's knowing i
hand over the short wick flickering
light of his life i hear him plead
his hands bound in white mitts
along the steel bars, his eyes
full of the sky and the traffic sounds
overhead the twin night suns
chrome bars moving down the
freeway down the hallway the
leaping shadows of small animals
of his arms of tree branches
flitting from this dream of flesh
the wind saying "such a long
time" his last words on the
telephone "till wednesday"

the leaves in the forest make
rain noises as they fall i feel the
dry rain brittle in my eyes falling
into my lungs, my lungs, he cried
straining in his hospital bed
on this forest floor brown and
sandy as his hair i lie down
on dead grass the autumn moss
creeping over my limbs strapping
me down strange rules and intricate
twistings the soil is formed of
fallen leaves will this too be
a blanket can i love enough now to
watch him live or die without knowing

how or why can i sit in this forest
as one of a billion fallen leaves
will this telling ever green
fresh tolerance through a forest
grown sick with jealousy? there's

no key to the closed door our
hands clawing on the rising hull
will you bring him back will you
let him into the ark will you
let me into the ark will you
flood my mind with clues to this
trick you're playing i
hear the music but where
have all the children gone
the receptionist typing, orderlies
pushing things on wheels i hear
anonymous feet in the waiting room
the sound of many flowers crying i
must let this go now, it is your
rule, not mine, you have declared
that your surrounding is released
by my surrendering you have dangled
us upside down you made this toy
world and wound us up to shed tears
if i refuse to cry now refuse to
play in your wind-up world refuse
to laugh at the trick if i refuse
if i say no say no

but it's dark here wednesday
never comes my hands uprooted my
hands crumbling i'll put down this
pen as well i'll wait by this

empty no longer with me river this
white breeze in a soundless
forest without trees

you recede with the softness of
layers of gauze here where the
not yet shadow falls quiet
as the moon i watch you
fleeing the thick wave

this abandoning this abandonment
crawls with love

from *Jericho Road*

Fish Poem

moving into the slow
pool beneath the voices
to the quiet garden where
airtime sounds are
cloud shadow and
sun games – what
matters here in this cool
inverted sky are small
darting fish
coloured cues shimmering
past the hooks, beneath
the nets, succulent, safe
and swift as prayer

from *Woman in the Woods*

Ant and Bee Poem

love i say meaning
glue as in i
glue you to
everything – the
sky the kitchen
cupboard – i glue you
to this letter that
i seal with moist
tongue and love
i say meaning
food as in
send me your
round nubby words
to taste the sweet
chewy texture of
honeycomb wax
and love i say
meaning hunger and
this flung apart
longing and the busy
ants on the cupboard wall
carrying bits of sweet wax
home

from *Woman in the Woods*

As Though It Were the Earth

as though it were the earth
and the words were hoes, shovels
garden tools stacked at
eden's gates – i will
talk about love –
spade the earth bury my face
in the soil search for you everywhere
since each time we begin to meet
the angel stands flaming sword in hand

since words have dripped
open from the fruit's wound
and been planted in our limbs
and each wounding brings
a fresh outpouring

until the swords are withdrawn
or we wrench them free
until the words cease
until the wounding ends

from *Jericho Road*

Wilber to the Dawn
(for Wilber Sutherland 1924-1997)

and so, dear friend,
still bound as we are here
by tides of human bonding
we have gathered to applaud
the journeying

and you
who, so far as i can tell
from heaven came
and to heaven have gone
and while on earth
made heaven home

from living room to living
room you go
while we in this garden
or that, as mary sat
in various states of unbelief
wait for the great
surprise

how happily you lived
without disguise
in all your every moment
book filled speaking days
in boat or beach or tent
or auditorium, in church
and synagogue and meeting room
and deeply in the words and
ready arms, wilber
with your eagerness to
serve

you did that
hour by faithful hour
and with such willingness of heart
in the service of your truths
and of the god we both call
love

within this universe, i pray
you still move, you live
and have your being in this same
element of love where we
this side of eden
toil

until like you, to the tomb
we come, that
busiest place of the
holiest one
in the journey to death
that is wholly
undone

wilber of the onward way
wilber to the dawn
i celebrate with these
your many loves
a well sung song
for you drank freely,
again, so far as i can tell
from the sweetest well

Dance Lesson

the dance master
dances in the tunnels
in the bone marrow –
crippled, he cries
that any awkward step
must do

here then and here are
these gentle deformed ones
holding the limbs
of the swaying sounds

how beautifully music
moves in the air
with the dance master naming
our names like a song

from *Woman in the Woods*

Water Song

that once
on water walked
on water still
walks he
in atmosphere
so dense in miracle
we here find fins
for flying

from *Woman in the Woods*